Instant HTML5 Responsive Table Design How-to

Present your data everywhere on any device using responsive design techniques

Fernando Monteiro

PUBLISHING

BIRMINGHAM - MUMBAI

Instant HTML5 Responsive Table Design How-to

First published: April 2013

Production Reference: 1180413

Published by Packt Publishing Ltd.
Livery Place
35 Livery Street
Birmingham B3 2PB, UK.

ISBN 978-1-84969-726-2

www.packtpub.com

Credits

Author
Fernando Monteiro

Reviewers
Melanie Archer

David Lender

Alex Libby

Acquisition Editor
Martin Bell

Commissioning Editors
Sruthi Kutty

Meeta Rajani

Technical Editors
Sharvari Baet

Kaustubh S. Mayekar

Project Coordinator
Joel Goveya

Proofreaders
Mario Cecere

Maria Gould

Production Coordinator
Prachali Bhiwandkar

Cover Work
Prachali Bhiwandkar

Cover Image
Sheetal Aute

About the Author

Fernando Monteiro is a frontend developer, speaker, and mind behind the Responsive Boilerplate, micro framework for responsive layouts. He contributes several articles and materials on his blog and for the entire community of web design and development.

He is passionate about web standards, semantics, and mobile design.

He began his career as a graphic designer in 2004 and quickly became an expert in QuarkXPress, producing and editing more than 500 ads for different companies in different magazines.

He has worked as a manager of e-commerce and UX designer for various companies and products, including mobile applications. Since 2009 he has worked full time as a frontend developer; his spare time is dedicated to open source projects and freelance jobs.

I would like to thank everyone who supported me in this journey, to Ellen for all the moments of encouragement, my son Mateus for always being by my side, and my whole family; it is impossible to mention them all here.

All the staff from PackPub who had contact directly with me in this incredible opportunity; thanks for all the patience and support.

About the Reviewers

Melanie Archer is a web developer living in Oakland, California, USA. Since handcoding her first web page in 1997, she's worked with many corporations, design agencies, and startups to bring standards-compliant delight to dozens of user interfaces. Other Packt titles she has reviewed include *HTML5 Boilerplate Web Development*, Divya Manian. You can follow Melanie on Twitter at @mejarc.

David Lender has been designing websites for over 13 years. He was an early adopter of HTML5, CSS3, and Responsive Design. He currently works at Washington University in St Louis as a Senior Project Leader of the SharePoint Design Group. He also works as a freelance Web Designer and has a personal website/blog at http://davidlender.com. In his spare time, he practices and helps teach Tae Kwon Do at Champion Martial Arts and is a second-degree black belt.

> I would like thank my beautiful wife, Tina, who has been a driving force of love and patience to me in our marriage, and my great kids. And in no particular order, great friends who have been more like family to me: Michelle King, Jeff King, Denise Prinkey, Tim Prinkey, Herbie Garcia, Krista Garcia, and Greg Phillips.

Alex Libby works in IT support. He has been involved in supporting end users for the last 15 years in a variety of different environments, and he currently works as a Technical Analyst/Solutions Architect, supporting a medium-sized SharePoint estate for an international parts distributor based in the UK. Although he gets to play with different technologies in his day job, his first true love has always been with the open source movement, and in particular, experimenting with CSS3, HTML5, and jQuery. To date, he has written several books for Packt Publishing, including one on HTML5 Video and another on jQuery tools.

www.PacktPub.com

Support files, eBooks, discount offers and more

You might want to visit www.PacktPub.com for support files and downloads related to your book.

Did you know that Packt offers eBook versions of every book published, with PDF and ePub files available? You can upgrade to the eBook version at www.PacktPub.com and as a print book customer, you are entitled to a discount on the eBook copy. Get in touch with us at service@packtpub.com for more details.

At www.PacktPub.com, you can also read a collection of free technical articles, sign up for a range of free newsletters and receive exclusive discounts and offers on Packt books and eBooks.

http://PacktLib.PacktPub.com

Do you need instant solutions to your IT questions? PacktLib is Packt's online digital book library. Here, you can access, read and search across Packt's entire library of books.

Why Subscribe?
- ▶ Fully searchable across every book published by Packt
- ▶ Copy and paste, print and bookmark content
- ▶ On demand and accessible via web browser

Free Access for Packt account holders

If you have an account with Packt at www.PacktPub.com, you can use this to access PacktLib today and view nine entirely free books. Simply use your login credentials for immediate access.

Table of Contents

Preface

We all know the importance of good design for the success of a product, service, or even a simple website. Serving our content on different platforms, systems, and different screen sizes has been more common than you might imagine.

There are infinite web frameworks that help us in this process, but there is nothing better than getting your hands dirty and learning to make these yourself.

Fortunately, we have several techniques that help us in this field that are so fascinating in web development. With the new implementation of HTML5, CSS3 Media Queries, and the massive evolution of JavaScript, our challenges can be overcome with more efficiency.

But not everything is perfect, and we can find some obstacles along the way; data tables are a good example, especially when they contain complex information or simply a large number of rows and columns.

What should we do to show large amounts of tabular data on a small-screen device?

How do we deal with this kind of problem and write tables using semantic tags such as: `caption`, `thead`, `tfoot`, and `tbody`?

This book will be your step-by-step guide in building responsive tables optimized for small screens, with some responsive design techniques and the use of some open source tools that will make our tables more pleasant and beautiful.

We will see how to turn tables into graphs and finally how we feed our tables using a basic JavaScript to load its content directly from a JSON file.

If you've heard about responsive design, or already have some knowledge in this area and want to explore the features available, this book is for you.

Here you will discover how you can implement complex tables with just a few lines of code.

If you do not know any techniques of responsive design, do not worry, the examples shown in the book are self explanatory and you will understand them.

Enjoy!

What this book covers

Throughout this book, we'll understand what elements make up a basic table and add some tags to improve the semantics of your code, also we'll use some JavaScript (or a jQuery Plugin) and JSON techniques to enhance the presentation, in addition you will be prepared to face the following challenges:

Introducing the new HTML5 table (Simple) gives an introduction to tables from a simple table to a semantic complex table using `caption`, `thead`, `tfoot`, `tbody` and `scope`. We also used some CSS properties to style our table and make it more pleasant to our eyes. And last but not the least, we will see how to deal with tables in a user experience perspective with some tips.

Understanding responsive web design (Simple) helps us understand how responsive design works, and which elements we use to make our tables responsive. A brief overview of the possible difficulties of handling tables responsively in small screens.

Getting started with responsive tables (Intermediate) explains the populating of a table with text and using some CSS3 Media Queries and a jQuery plugin to help you select some columns and apply filters to display the most relevant information to your users.

Dealing with numbers (Intermediate) explains how to load data using a JSON file with a few lines of JavaScript and jQuery as our table is correctly formatted.

Increasing the numbers (advanced) explains what happens when we increased the amount of data and introduced a small JavaScript library to improve the compatibility of some CSS3 properties not yet supported by all browsers.

Converting tables into graphs (Advanced) explains what happens when we convert the data and display a nice graphic for our users using a properly formatted table.

Merging data – numbers and text (Advanced) explains tables with numbers and texts are more common than you can imagine, using a few lines of JavaScript and a jQuery plugin, manipulate the data and apply filters by columns.

Mixing everything – texts, numbers and more data helps us organize our table and share data to optimize viewing and loading the table into smaller devices. Adding break points in our stylesheet for better consistency in different screen sizes.

What you need for this book

All examples in the book use open source solutions and can be downloaded for free on the links provided in each recipe, however you may choose to use their own tools.

The book's examples use the JavaScript library jQuery 1.8.3, the most current version when writing this book, which can be downloaded for free here: `http://jquery.com/download/`.

The text editor called Sublime Text 2 can be found at `http://www.sublimetext/2`.

Also we made use of some small libraries (Polyfill) to help us with a better presentation in old browsers, that is "helps outdated browsers interpret new tags":

- ▶ `- HTML5 - https://raw.github.com/aFarkas/html5shiv/master/src/html5shiv.js`
- ▶ `- Media Queries - https://raw.github.com/scottjehl/Respond/master/respond.min.js`

A modern browser will be very helpful too, we use Chrome, but feel free to use whichever you prefer, we recommend one of these: Safari, Firefox, Chrome, IE, and Opera and these are all in their latest versions.

A simple tool to change your browser size just for the development process, we use a Chrome extension and you can find it here:

`https://chrome.google.com/webstore/detail/window-resizer/kkelicaakdanhinjdeammmilcgefonfh`

Even this solution is not the perfect but using this case is faster and cheaper than having several devices for testing.

And finally, we use a web server to process our JSON file and load it without problems.

We recommend using the Mongoose Server, as it is being very light and simple to use.

`http://code.google.com/p/mongoose/downloads/list`

Also if you need some help with the markup you can download the code examples.

Who this book is for

If you're new to the world of responsive design techniques and want to explore the functionality available to style your tables and optimize its use for small-screen devices, this book is for you.

You must have a basic to intermediate knowledge of HTML, CSS, and jQuery, to follow the examples in the book, but a slightly more advanced knowledge of jQuery/JavaScript may be required in some recipes. Do not worry about it, the examples will detail all the code. Remember that we focus on the presentation of tabular data and all our examples are made in this form.

Conventions

In this book, you will find a number of styles of text that distinguish between different kinds of information. Here are some examples of these styles, and an explanation of their meaning.

Code words in text are shown as follows: "We can include other contexts through the use of the `include` directive."

A block of code is set as follows:

```
<table>
    <tr>
        <td>Band</td>
        <td>Album</td>
    </tr>
</table>
```

When we wish to draw your attention to a particular part of a code block, the relevant lines or items are set in bold:

```
<table>
    <tr>
        <th>Band</th>
        <td>Album</td>
    </tr>
</table>
```

New terms and **important words** are shown in bold. Words that you see on the screen, in menus or dialog boxes for example, appear in the text like this: "Clicking the **Next** button moves you to the next screen".

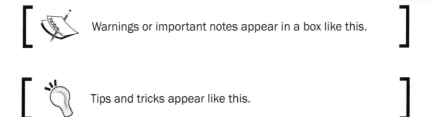

Warnings or important notes appear in a box like this.

Tips and tricks appear like this.

Reader feedback

Feedback from our readers is always welcome. Let us know what you think about this book—what you liked or may have disliked. Reader feedback is important for us to develop titles that you really get the most out of.

To send us general feedback, simply send an e-mail to feedback@packtpub.com, and mention the book title via the subject of your message.

If there is a book that you need and would like to see us publish, please send us a note in the **SUGGEST A TITLE** form on www.packtpub.com or e-mail suggest@packtpub.com.

If there is a topic that you have expertise in and you are interested in either writing or contributing to a book, see our author guide on www.packtpub.com/authors.

Customer support

Now that you are the proud owner of a Packt book, we have a number of things to help you to get the most from your purchase.

Downloading the example code

You can download the example code files for all Packt books you have purchased from your account at `http://www.PacktPub.com`. If you purchased this book elsewhere, you can visit `http://www.PacktPub.com/support` and register to have the files e-mailed directly to you.

Errata

Although we have taken every care to ensure the accuracy of our content, mistakes do happen. If you find a mistake in one of our books—maybe a mistake in the text or the code—we would be grateful if you would report this to us. By doing so, you can save other readers from frustration and help us improve subsequent versions of this book. If you find any errata, please report them by visiting `http://www.packtpub.com/support`, selecting your book, clicking on the **errata submission form** link, and entering the details of your errata. Once your errata are verified, your submission will be accepted and the errata will be uploaded on our website, or added to any list of existing errata, under the Errata section of that title. Any existing errata can be viewed by selecting your title from `http://www.packtpub.com/support`.

Piracy

Piracy of copyright material on the Internet is an ongoing problem across all media. At Packt, we take the protection of our copyright and licenses very seriously. If you come across any illegal copies of our works, in any form, on the Internet, please provide us with the location address or website name immediately so that we can pursue a remedy.

Please contact us at `copyright@packtpub.com` with a link to the suspected pirated material.

We appreciate your help in protecting our authors, and our ability to bring you valuable content.

Questions

You can contact us at `questions@packtpub.com` if you are having a problem with any aspect of the book, and we will do our best to address it.

Instant HTML5 Responsive Table Design How-to

Welcome to *Instant HTML5 Responsive Table Design How-to*. This book covers how to optimize and visualize your data using responsive design techniques. It also demonstrates a simple and effective way to treat your data in different screen sizes.

Introducing the new HTML5 table (Simple)

A simple table is basically composed of the `<table>`, `<tr>`, and `<td>` tags. Besides this, its contents should also make sense if you remove these tags. Hence you should have a clear understanding of its contents.

With the use of additional elements such as `caption`, `thead`, `tbody`, and `tfooter`, we have a **data table**, that is two or more dimensions. Each data cell `<td>` needs to be represented by a minimum of two unique vertices for the `<th>` headings.

Also, the table needs to be structured so that when it is rendered, for each row there are the same number of columns.

Using these elements we can maintain our table with a semantic code. As mentioned in the W3C Candidate Recommendation for tabular data (dated 17 December 2012), it is not mandatory to close `<thead>`, `<tr>`, `<th>`, `<td>`, and `<tbody>` tags.

Getting ready

Before we see the difference in the code, let's see a simple table. Remember, every table requires a minimum markup to be valid, it should have at least the `<table>`, `<tr>` and `<td>` tags. The following screenshot shows a simple table without any stylesheet:

Band	Album
Ac/Dc	Back in Black
Deep Purple Burn	

Band Album Ac/Dc Back in Black Deep Purple Burn

Table 01

Now we use a more complex markup with the `<caption>`, `<thead>`, `<tbody>`, and `<tfooter>` tags. In order to achieve a better visual result, we apply some lines of CSS. The following screenshot shows a table with a basic stylesheet:

CLASSIC ALBUMS OF THE EIGHTIES			
BAND	ALBUM	CLASSIC	YEAR
AC/DC	Back in Black	Back in Black	1980
Van Hallen	1984	Jump	1984
Bruce Springsteen	Nebraska	Hungry Heart	1982
* Some research font goes here just for the example.			

Table 02

How to do it...

Here we assume that you already have the minimum markup of an HTML5 document formatted, but if you prefer open the example (*Chapter01_Codes*) of the book and follow the code:

1. First insert the minimum markup necessary to create a table.

2. Then we use the `<caption>`, `<thead>`, and `<tbody>` elements to give us more flexibility in styling the table.

3. And finally apply the style to format the table and improve the visualization as follows:

```
<!--Very basic Table layout-->
<table>
<tr>
<td>Band</td>
<td>Album</td>
  </tr>
<tr>
```

```
<td>Ac/Dc</td>
<td>Back in Black</td>
</tr>
<tr>
<td>Deep Purple</td>
<td>Burn</td>
</tr>
</table>
```

4. Now we add the new elements to the HTML document:

```
<!--This div is only to create a border around the table -->
<div class="container">
  <table class="table">
    <caption>CLASSIC ALBUMS OF THE EIGHTIES</caption>
    <thead>
    <tr>
    <th scope="col">BAND</th>
    <th scope="col">ALBUM</th>
    <th scope="col">CLASSIC</th>
    <th scope="col">YEAR</th>
    </tr>
    </thead>
    <tfoot>
    <tr>
    <td colspan="4">* Some research font goes here just for the
example.</td>
    </tr>
    </tfoot>
    <tbody>
    <tr>
    <th scope="row">AC/DC</th>
    <td>Back in Black</td>
    <td>Back in Black</td>
    <td>1980</td>
    </tr>
    <tr>
    <th scope="row">Van Hallen</th>
    <td>1984</td>
    <td>Jump</td>
    <td>1984</td>
    </tr>
    <tr>
    <th scope="row">Bruce Springsteen</th>
    <td>Nebraska</td>
```

```
      <td>Hungry Heart</td>
      <td>1982</td>
      </tr>
      <tbody>
    </table>
  </div>
```

5. And finally, we add the CSS rules to our table as follows:

```
.container {
    width:600px;
    overflow: hidden;
    border:1px solid #000;
}
.table {
    background-color: transparent;
    border-collapse: collapse;
    border-spacing: 0;
    background-color: #fff;
}
.table th,
.table td {
    padding: 8px;
    line-height: 20px;
    text-align: left;
    vertical-align: top;
    border-top: 1px solid #dddddd;
}
.table th {
    font-weight: bold;
}
.table thead th {
    vertical-align: bottom;
    color:#0006ff;
}
```

The result is what we saw in screenshot, *Table 02*.

For the purposes of this book, the CSS code was embedded in the header of our page as you can see in the code examples.

 In a production environment, you should serve your stylesheets separately from your HTML code. (For performance reasons and to follow good standards of development, we recommend this procedure.)

How it works...

With the addition of new elements, you can easily stylize your table only using the `<thead>` and `<th>` selectors. Note that we add the `.table` class just for demonstration.

This is a very simple style, but our markup is semantic and our code can be easily interpreted by the screen readers. With the aid of the `<scope>` tag, we can define the individual headers for each column as follows:

```
<tr>
    <th scope="col">BAND</th>
    <th scope="col">ALBUM</th>
    <th scope="col">CLASSIC</th>
    <th scope="col">YEAR</th>
</tr>
```

And apply the blue color to all our headers as you can see in *Table 02*.

There's more...

The `<scope>` syntax is very intuitive and is written as follows:

```
<th scope="col|row|colgroup|rowgroup">
```

The preceding syntax is explained as follows:

- `col` – The header cell is a header for a column
- `row` – The header cell is a header for row
- `colgroup` – The header cell is a header for group of columns
- `rowgroup` – The header cell is a header for group of rows

Some useful user experience tips about tables

Let's take a look at the tables by the User Experience Design perspective:

- Always give abbreviations for numbers and names as it's unnecessary to display every digit of a number. You can abbreviate large numbers such as $250,000 to $250k and large names such as John Doe Novatto to John Doe.
- Tooltips are welcome too. It helps the users see the real and full value for each field.
- Keep headers fixed on table scrolling. It's hard for users to know what the information they're looking at is, without seeing the column header. See line 125 for example.

- ▸ Differentiate their lines with different colors (zebra stripes), extensive tables are very easy to get confused when you look at certain lines.

- ▸ Get used to using the `<caption>` tag to describe the contents of your tables, it is very important for accessibility because screen readers identify this information and use the `<scope>` tag to associate the cells with the headers.

Of course, this list has a few tips but you can search more info on the web.

Accessibility tip

Use of the `<th>` and `<scope>` tags combined with the `<caption>` and `<summary>` tags will provide sufficient information for most newer screen readers to process simple tables.

A good resource for accessibility can be found here at `http://accessibility.psu.edu/wcag2`.

Understanding responsive web design (Simple)

Responsive web design requires a very different way of thinking about layout that is both challenging and exciting. First we must base our layout in fluid grids, that is we should use percentages instead of pixels.

This way we can have greater control over the width of the elements positioned on the screen. This is one of the basic principles of responsive layout. There are two other important aspects that help us deal with this development technique but both are outside the scope of our book. You can find more information by visiting the following link:

`http://en.wikipedia.org/wiki/Responsive_web_design`

Getting ready

With this information it would be very simple to think that we can set the width of our table in percentages and that our problems are solved, right? Wrong or not exactly right, let's go back to our table in the last recipe and add more columns to make a simple verification.

How to do it...

Let's open the example code, *Chapter02_Codes*.

1. Now we add four `<th>` tags to the `<thead>` tag.
2. Then add more four `<td>` to each `<tr>` on the table body.
3. Finally, add a border to the container div on our CSS.

4. Here's our HTML code with four more columns:

```
<div class="container">
  <table>
    <caption>CLASSIC ALBUMS OF THE EIGHTIES</caption>
    <thead>
    <tr>
    <th scope="col">BAND</th>
    <th scope="col">ALBUM</th>
    <th scope="col">CLASSIC</th>
    <th scope="col">YEAR</th>
    <th scope="col">SALES 1981</th>
    <th scope="col">SALES 1982</th>
    <th scope="col">SALES 1983</th>
    <th scope="col">SALES 1984</th>
    </tr>
    </thead>
    <tfoot>
    <tr>
    <td colspan="8">* This table is only for example purposes and
don't express the really.</td>
    </tr>
    </tfoot>
    <tbody>
    <tr>
    <th scope="row">AC/DC</th>
    <td>Back in Black</td>
    <td>Back in Black</td>
    <td>1980</td>
    <td>120.000</td>
    <td>60.000</td>
    <td>10.000</td>
    <td>130.000</td>
    </tr>
    <tr>
    <th scope="row">Van Hallen</th>
    <td>1984</td>
    <td>Jump</td>
    <td>1984</td>
    <td>0</td>
    <td>0</td>
    <td>0</td>
    <td>120.000</td>
    </tr>
    <tr>
```

```
            <th scope="row">Bruce Springsteen</th>
            <td>Nebraska</td>
            <td>Hungry Heart</td>
            <td>1982</td>
            <td>0</td>
            <td>60.000</td>
            <td>70.000</td>
            <td>120.000</td>
            </tr>
            <tbody>
      </table>
      </div>
```

We can use more than eight columns but this is enough for our example.

Downloading the example code

You can download the example code files for all Packt books you have purchased from your account at http://www.packtpub.com. If you purchased this book elsewhere, you can visit http://www.packtpub.com/support and register to have the files e-mailed directly to you.

5. Add a border to the div container, as we see here:

```
.container {
    width:980px;
    overflow: hidden;
    border:1px solid #000;
}
```

How it works...

When our div container is 600px, our table is good but when we change the container width to 980px (*Table 03*), our table is still safe but does not occupy the entire space of the container, as shown in the following screenshot (note the blank space on right side):

CLASSIC ALBUMS OF THE EIGHTIES							
BAND	ALBUM	CLASSIC	YEAR	SALES 1981	SALES 1982	SALES 1983	SALES 1984
AC/DC	Back in Black	Back in Black	1980	120.000	60.000	10.000	130.000
Van Hallen	1984	Jump	1984	0	0	0	120.000
Bruce Springsteen	Nebraska	Hungry Heart	1982	0	60.000	70.000	120.000
* This table is only for example purposes and don't express the really.							

Table 03

Now let's see what happens when we add 100 percent of width on our table:

CLASSIC ALBUMS OF THE EIGHTIES							
BAND	ALBUM	CLASSIC	YEAR	SALES 1981	SALES 1982	SALES 1983	SALES 1984
AC/DC	Back in Black	Back in Black	1980	120.000	60.000	10.000	130.000
Van Hallen	1984	Jump	1984	0	0	0	120.000
Bruce Springsteen	Nebraska	Hungry Heart	1982	0	60.000	70.000	120.000
* This table is only for example purposes and don't express the reality.							

Table 04: Table with 100 percent width

A little better than the previous one, in this case it is not really a problem, but imagine if our div decreased instead of increasing?

For this, from now to the end of the book we'll use some Media Queries techniques to help us with small screen devices.

There's more...

This matter being outside the scope of this book, we recommend reading the w3c article at `http://www.w3.org/TR/css3-mediaqueries/` for better understanding of how this method of development works.

Media queries, which are part of the CSS3 draft spec, don't work in Internet Explorer 6, 7, or 8, Firefox 3, and Opera 9. Hardly surprising, but certainly annoying. So, we need a JavaScript solution for older browsers.

Here's a link to a useful resource to check browsers' support:

`http://www.caniause.com`

The following screenshot shows the media queries' browser compatibility:

CSS3 Media Queries - Recommendation

Method of applying styles based on media information. Includes things like page and device dimensions

Usage stats:		Global
Support:		83.63%
Partial support:		0.02%
Total:		83.65%

Show all versions	IE	Firefox	Chrome	Safari	Opera	iOS Safari	Opera Mini	Android Browser	Blackberry Browser
								2.1	
						3.2		2.2	
	7.0					4.0-4.1		2.3	
	8.0	15.0				4.2-4.3		3.0	
	9.0	16.0	22.0	5.1		5.0-5.1		4.0	
Current	10.0	17.0	23.0	6.0	12.1	6.0	5.0-7.0	4.1	7.0
Near future		18.0	24.0		12.5				10.0
Farther future		19.0	25.0						

Some lines about Polyfills

For the next recipes we introduce a small library called `Respond.js` also known as **Polyfill** to help us with media queries in outdated browsers.

This script simply scans the CSS files for the queries, and then implements them as normal CSS when the page is resized. It's a simple enough idea but the code itself is reasonably complex; it actually loads the external CSS files using AJAX, and herein lies the rub.

You can read more about this at `http://en.wikipedia.org/wiki/Polyfill`.

Getting started with responsive tables (Intermediate)

Now that we already know how to run a responsive layout, let's dive into this challenging field and use some CSS3 properties to give a better design and look to our table.

Getting ready

First add the following lines at the bottom of the HTML page:

```
<!-- JavaScript at the bottom for fast page loading with just one js
file -->
  <script src="http://ajax.googleapis.com/ajax/libs/jquery/1.8.3/
jquery.min.js"></script>
  <script src="https://raw.github.com/scottjehl/Respond/master/
respond.min.js"></script>
```

How to do it...

Open the example file, *Chapter03_Codes_1*. We need to apply our CSS to make a responsive table as follows:

1. Add a round corner to our `container` class with `border-radius` and use `max-width` to increase the `container` width to `800px`.

2. Use the browser vendor prefix (`-moz` and `-webkit`) to make some browsers understand gradient CSS property.

3. Add another new feature from CSS3, `box-shadow`.

4. Use pseudo-classes `nth-child(odd)` and `nth-child(even)` to "zebra" the table rows as follows:

```
        .container {
            max-width: 800px;
            margin: 0 auto;
```

```css
        font-family: 'Crimison Text', Arial, sans-serif;
        padding: 0.5em 1em 1em 1em;

        border-radius: 10px;

        background-color: #808080;
        background: -webkit-gradient(linear, left top, left
bottom, from(#333), to(#ccc));
        background: -moz-linear-gradient(top, #606060,
#808080);

        -moz-box-shadow: 5px 5px 10px rgba(0,0,0,0.3);
        -webkit-box-shadow: 5px 5px 10px rgba(0,0,0,0.3);
        box-shadow: 5px 5px 10px rgba(0,0,0,0.3);
    }
    h1 {color:#fff; font-size:1.5em; text-align: center;}
    table.tableCss3 {
        width: 100%;
        border-collapse:collapse;
        text-align:left;
        color: #000000;
    }
    table.tableCss3 thead tr td {
        background-color: White;
        vertical-align:middle;
        padding: 0.6em;
        font-size:0.8em;
    }
    table.tableCss3 thead tr th {
        padding: 0.5em;
        /* add gradient */
        background-color: #bdbdbd;
        background: -webkit-gradient(linear, left top, left
bottom, from(#d6d6d6), to(#bdbdbd));
        background: -moz-linear-gradient(top, #d6d6d6,
#bdbdbd);
        color: #000000;
    }
    table.tableCss3 tbody tr:nth-child(odd) {
        background-color: #fafafa;
    }
    table.tableCss3 tbody tr:nth-child(odd):hover {
        cursor:pointer;
        /* add gradient */
```

```
            background-color: #fafafa;
            background: -webkit-gradient(linear, left top, left
    bottom, from(#fafafa), to(#e0e0e0));
            background: -moz-linear-gradient(top, #fafafa,
    #e0e0e0);
            color: #333;
        }
        table.tableCss3 tbody tr:nth-child(even) {
            background-color: #efefef;
        }
        table.tableCss3 tbody tr:nth-child(even):hover {
            cursor:pointer;
            /* add gradient */
            background-color: #808080;
            background: -webkit-gradient(linear, left top, left
    bottom, from(#e0e0e0), to(#f1f1f1));
            background: -moz-linear-gradient(top, #ebebeb,
    #f7f7f7);
            color: #333;
        }
        table.tableCss3 tbody tr:last-child {
            border-bottom: solid 1px #838383;
        }
        table.tableCss3 td {
          vertical-align:middle;
          padding: 0.5em;
        }
        table.tableCss3 tfoot{
          text-align:center;
          color:#303030;
          text-shadow: 0 1px 1px rgba(255,255,255,0.3);
        }
```

5. We set max-width of the container to 800px and width of the table to 100% to adjust the table width to all screen size. The 800px from div container is only for the example here but can be of any size.

6. After incorporating these minimal changes, our table is shown throughout our browser.

We add a `.tableCss3` class just to illustrate the new CSS3 selectors and pseudo-classes.

The preceding screenshot is of the browser at 1024 px – 768 px.

7. And when we resize the browser window, our table adjusts to fit their new size:

The preceding screenshot is of the browser at 320px – 480px.

So far so good, but how can we improve this result with more columns?

We can filter the data columns that are less important to the user. But remember you should always allow your user `tp` to choose what is most important to him, so be flexible.

Find more information about CSS3 selector here: `http://www.w3.org/TR/selectors/#selectors`

There's more...

Browser prefix is a technique used in the stylesheets to warn browsers that have not yet implemented certain property that it is being used through a prefix placed before the property.

For example, `-ms` for Internet Explorer, `-webkit` for Safari and Chrome, and so on.

You will find a complete reference guide of prefixes and properties at `http://www.w3schools.com/cssref/css3_browsersupport.asp`.

Introduction to MediaTable plugin

In the following example, we will see how to apply a filter and select some columns to be displayed in smaller devices, and gradually show all columns in larger devices.

We'll use the example code, *Chapter03_Codes_2*.

Hands on and add the following tag to the bottom of our file:

```
<script src="https://raw.github.com/thepeg/MediaTable/master/jquery.
mediaTable.js">
</script>
```

Also, add the following script tag just after the preceding line of code:

```
<script>
  $(document).ready(function(){
    $('.mediaTable').mediaTable();
  });
</script>
```

Now add the following script to the head of our page, just after the `<style>` tag:

```
<link rel="stylesheet" type="text/css" media="all" href="mediatable.
css" />
```

Here is a short description of the code, it's a jQuery plugin that helps us with the table filters. We apply them to our columns, so this way we can give options to our users to filter the content themselves.

We can choose a solution using only pure JavaScript or even write a new jQuery plugin, but it is not necessary to reinvent the wheel.

 JavaScript is the fastest growing language today. We have an infinity of snippets and plugins available to us everyday, and a very active community.

We recommend that you do a little search on github at `https://github.com` and explore the endless existing codes on it.

Here's a very simple piece of code, we will add some classes to our markup just to prefilter some options and we will set some columns as `optional` and others as `essential`:

```
<tr>
<th scope="col" class="essential persist">BAND</th>
<th scope="col" class="essential">ALBUM</th>
<th scope="col" class="essential">CLASSIC</th>
<th scope="col" class="essential">YEAR</th>
<th scope="col" class="optional">SALES 1981</th>
<th scope="col" class="optional">SALES 1982</th>
<th scope="col" class="optional">SALES 1983</th>
<th scope="col" class="optional">SALES 1984</th>
</tr>
```

Now on resizing, we see the three essential columns and a link on top-right corner:

The preceding screenshot is of the browser at 320px.

When we press the link, we can see the filter, as shown in the following screenshot:

Browser screenshot at 320 px, now with the filter.

Note that we are not taking into account the height of the table, we are only considering the width. We will have the scroll bar down later and it does not affect the way in which we provide the data.

Some lines about breakpoints

After append `mediatable.css`, we introduce the breakpoints from our media queries. Breakpoints means that we can set a new size with a expression like this:

```
@media screen and (min-width: 768px) {...your code here}
```

This means that the style between the brackets will be interpreted by the browser if the screen resolution is less than `768px`. And the same will apply to any other resolution when we define our size in the min or max width.

 All responsive frameworks today use this technique to create their layouts based on fluid columns and breakpoints.

The most common breakpoints are 320px, 480px, 768px, and 1024px.

Dealing with numbers (Intermediate)

Let's look at another alternative now. How to deal with numerical tables? When dealing with responsive design it is strongly recommended that you develop your application from the bottom up, that is the smallest to the largest 320px to 1024px or 1280px to 1360px. This way of development is known as **mobile first**.

Getting ready

It is hard to imagine how to show a table with over 10 columns on such a small screen. Let's see a pretty interesting alternative. Using another trick with a jQuery Plugin called: **Footable.js**.

How to do it...

First let's take a look in our table:

BAND	MEMBERS	CREW	MONTH SHOWS	YEARS SHOWS	FANS	BEERS	FOODS
			TOUR COSTS				
AC/DC	4	10	8	80	60.000	10.000	130.000
Van Hallen	5	13	12	120	60.000	120	120.000
Bruce Springsteen	6	18	16	130	60.000	6.000	180.000
Metallica	4	25	18	250	60.000	200.000	180.000

* This table is only for example purposes and don't express the reality.

Full width table of 1024px

Now on resizing, we have something like an accordion:

Browser resized at 320px

When we click on the table header, we see the other rows, as shown in the following screenshot:

TOUR COSTS

BAND

AC/DC

MEMBERS : 4
CREW : 10
MONTH SHOWS : 8
YEARS SHOWS : 80
FANS : 60.000
BEERS : 10.000
FOODS : 130.000

Van Hallen

Bruce Springsteen

Metallica

* This table is only for example purposes and don't express the reality.

Accordion behavior when the header is clicked

The following are steps required to complete this task, you can use the code examples (*Chapter04_Codes_1*):

1. Add some extra CSS lines to our markup.

2. Include the stylesheet plugin to the head of page.

3. Insert the JavaScript plugin to the bottom of our page.

4. And finally, initiate the plugin with a jQuery function.

5. Now we going into the magic, let's see our changes on css:

```
.table tbody tr:nth-child(odd) td,
.table tbody tr:nth-child(odd) th {
  background-color: #f9f9f9;
```

```
        }
    .table tbody tr:hover td,
    .table tbody tr:hover th {
       background-color: whitesmoke;
    }
```

6. In the head of our page, include a stylesheet link to the plugin's CSS:

```
<link rel="stylesheet" type="text/css" media="all" href="https://
raw.github.com/bradvin/FooTable/master/css/footable-0.1.css" />
```

7. Add the plugin's link to the bottom of the page right after the jQuery:

```
<script src="https://raw.github.com/bradvin/FooTable/master/js/
footable-0.1.js"></script>
```

8. Finally, invoke the jQuery function to make the magic happen:

```
<script type="text/javascript">
    $(function() {
       $('.table').footable();
    });
</script>
```

There's more...

We will see a way to load the data from your table through a JSON file and a few lines of JavaScript and jQuery.

You can even use this snippet of code into their applications, code example *Chapter04_Codes_2.*

 Here we need to publish our HTML file on a web server, otherwise you might not been able to see the result when you load the JSON file in your browser due to **Access-Control-Allow-Origin**.

Here you can use the **Mongoose Server** included in the codes examples, or download it from the link provided on our *Preface*.

Just go to downloaded codes folder and execute the server with a double click, now open your browser and type `http://localhost:8080`. This is the default port for Mongoose but if you already have your port 8080 busy, just right-click on the Mongoose icon present at the bottom toolbar and choose **Edit Config File** and change the port.

Check out the JavaScript code:

```javascript
// Build the table from a Json file
$.getJSON('table_content_2.json', function(data) {

    var table = $('#dynamicTable');

    var trthead = $('<tr/>');

    var head = $('<thead/>');

    trthead.appendTo(head);

    //Loop over the columns
    $.each(data.listColumns, function (index, value) {
        var column = $('<th>' + value.Title + '</th>');
        trthead.append(column);
    });

    var tbody = $('<tbody/>');

    //Loop over the rows;
    for (var i = 0; i < data.listRows.length; i++) {
        var tr = $('<tr/>');
            for (var t = 0; t < data.listRows[i].Value.
length; t++) {

    if(t == 0){
        tr.append('<th>' + data.listRows[i].Value[t] + '</th>');
    }else{
        tr.append('<td>' + data.listRows[i].Value[t] + '</td>');
    }


        }

        tbody.append(tr);
    }
        table.append(head);
        table.append(tbody);
});
```

It is a simple yet functional code and can be applied to any type of table. Following this basic JSON structure, add the table markup on the document body:

```html
<table id="dynamicTable" class="table"></table>
```

On the body of your document add the script on the bottom, after the jQuery script.

Here's our JSON file:

```
{
    "listColumns": [
        {"Title": "Column 01", "id": 1},
        {"Title": "Column 02", "id": 2},
        {"Title": "Column 03", "id": 3},
        {"Title": "Column 04", "id": 4},
        {"Title": "Column 05", "id": 5},
        {"Title": "Column 06", "id": 6}
    ],
    "listRows": [
        {"Value": ["0","0","0","0","0","0"]},
        {"Value": ["0","0","0","0","0","0"]},
        {"Value": ["0","0","0","0","0","0"]},
        {"Value": ["0","0","0","0","0","0"]},
        {"Value": ["0","0","0","0","0","0"]},
        {"Value": ["0","0","0","0","0","0"]}
    ]
}
```

Quick tip about JSON

Now we introduce the JSON validate tool called **jsonlint** and you can find here:

```
http://jsonlint.com/
```

Its operation is very simple, just copy and paste your code in the JSON address and click on **Validate**.

In addition to validating your code, this tool can still indents and makes the code more pleasing to our eyes.

Increasing the numbers (Advanced)

Now let's see another way of dealing with our data table, based only on CSS and loading data via JSON file using the `$.getJSON();` and `$.ajax();` methods. Remember that you can use this code in your work, we have carefully optimized it as the JSON loading is very fast and the JSON file is very lightweight.

Getting ready

First it is necessary to run our small web server so that our request to JSON file works perfectly.

We'll be using Chrome throughout this recipe, although you may prefer to use a different browser—the Origin null message that you may see applies only to Chrome. Also you can use Firefox or Internet Explorer browser if you prefer, but the "Origin null is not allowed by Access-Control-Allow-Origin" message is only for Chrome browser.

How to do it...

1. Start the Mongoose Server and go to `http://localhost:8080` on your browser.

2. Open the example file, *Chapter05_Codes_1* or follow the next steps.

3. Insert a breakpoint in our stylesheet, to be more exact, in the head of the page.

4. Place the new CSS rules inside the Media Queries brackets.

5. Now, just below the existing style, we add the new code.

6. Let's now add in the relevant styles, as highlighted:

```
table {
    max-width: 100%;
    background-color: transparent;
    border-collapse: collapse;
    border-spacing: 0;
    background-color: #fff
}
.table {
    width: 100%;
    margin-bottom: 20px;
}
.table th,
.table td {
    padding: 8px;
    line-height: 20px;
    text-align: left;
    vertical-align: top;
    border-top: 1px solid #dddddd;
}
.table th {
    font-weight: bold;
}
.table thead th {
    vertical-align: bottom;
    color:#0006ff;
}
```

```
.table tbody tr:nth-child(odd) td,
.table tbody tr:nth-child(odd) th {
    background-color: #f9f9f9;
}
.table tbody tr:hover td,
.table tbody tr:hover th {
    background-color: whitesmoke;
}

@media only screen and (max-width: 768px) { }


@media only screen and (max-width: 768px) {

    .table { display: block; position: relative; width: 100%; }
    .table thead { display: block; float: left; background-color:
#ccc; }
    .table tbody {
       display: block;
       width: auto;
       position: relative;
       overflow-x: auto;
       white-space: nowrap;
       }
    .table thead tr { display: block; }
    .table th { display: block; }
    .table tbody tr { display: inline-block; vertical-align: top;
}

    .table td { display: block; min-height: 1.25em; }

    table tbody tr { border-right: 1px solid #babcbf; }

}
```

7. Note that we use only a `max-width: 768px` for this example and it works fine for this purpose.

8. At this moment our page must look like this on full-browser resolution:

BANDS	BLACK SABBATH	WHITESNAKE	QUEEN	NAZARETH	VAN HALEN	SCORPIONS	DEEP PURPLE	DEF LEPPARD	AC/DC
Studio Hours	1.900 h	2.000 h	2.600 h	4.000 h	3.150 h	2.970 h	3.000 h	2.000 h	1.700 h
Studio Cost	$ 245.000	$ 490.000	$ 800.000	$ 330.090	$ 600.099	$ 256.000	$ 599.389	$ 890.000	$ 480.000
S. Last Year	300 h	900 h	3.900 h	2.800 h	1.600 h	2.000 h	1.000 h	3.700 h	1.000 h
S. C. Last Year	$ 345.000	$ 690.000	$ 200.000	$ 830.090	$ 130.099	$ 756.000	$ 354.389	$ 600.000	$ 200.000
Road Hours	600 h	1.200 h	1.700 h	1.660 h	2.000 h	200 h	400 h	1.034 h	1.990 h
Gas	200 L	250 L	300 L	250 L	350 L	600 L	200 L	640 L	470 L
L. Y. Road Hours	900 h	1.900 h	789 h	2.000 h	290 h	654 h	2.600 h	3.000 h	1.300 h
L. Y Gas	490 L	520 L	600 L	400 L	678 L	354 L	534 L	400 L	200 L

Screenshot at 1024px

9. When resized to 320px, we see the scroll bar just below the table:

BANDS	Studio Hours	Studio
BLACK SABBATH	1.900 h	$ 245.
WHITESNAKE	2.000 h	$ 490.
QUEEN	2.600 h	$ 800.
NAZARETH	4.000 h	$ 330.
VAN HALEN	3.150 h	$ 600.
SCORPIONS	2.970 h	$ 256.
DEEP PURPLE	3.000 h	$ 599..
DEF LEPPARD	2.000 h	$ 890.
AC/DC	1.700 h	$ 480.

Screenshot at 320px

How it works...

Not bad, in our Media Queries we apply the **display block** property and the **display inline-block** property to our table <tbody> in the <tr> section.

Thus we force the table to show like a block and shift the <thead> tag to the left-hand side forcing the body to behave like a div and present it with a scroll bar.

Lets take a look at our JavaScript using the $.getJSON() jQuery function:

```
$.getJSON('table_content_2.json', function(data) {
            var table = $('#dynamicTable');

            var trthead = $('<tr/>');

            var head = $('<thead/>');

            trthead.appendTo(head);

        //Loop over the columns
            $.each(data.listColumns, function (index, value) {
                var column = $('<th>' + value.Title + '</th>');
                trthead.append(column);
```

```
            });

        var tbody = $('<tbody/>');

    //Loop over the rows;
        for (var i = 0; i < data.listRows.length; i++) {
            var tr = $('<tr/>');
                for (var t = 0; t < data.listRows[i].Value.
length; t++) {

                        if(t == 0){
                            tr.append('<th>' + data.listRows[i].Value[t]
+ '</th>');
                        }else{
                            tr.append('<td>' + data.listRows[i].Value[t]
+ '</td>');
                        }

                }

            tbody.append(tr);
        }
        table.append(head);
        table.append(tbody);
    });
```

As stated earlier our JSON file is lightweight and very easy to be generated by any server-side language that you want to use.

But it is necessary to obey the naming conventions of columns and rows as shown in the following code snippet:

```
{
    "listColumns": [
        {
            "Title": "BANDS",
            "id": 1
        }
    ],
    "listRows": [
        {
            "Value": [
                "Studio Hours",
                "1.900 h"

            ]
        }

    ]
}
```

There's more

We will now cover some information about $.ajax() method:

Using the $. Ajax() method, we have even more flexibility to work with very large JSON files.

We can determine a **loading** to appear during our request (using the beforeSend function) and when the data is transferred we can remove it (using the complete function).

Additionally we have a function to handle any errors that prevent the loading of data from our table, code example, *Chapter05_Codes_2*.

```
$.ajax({
        type: 'GET',
        url: 'http://localhost:8080/table_content_2.json',
        timeout: 5000,
        dataType: "json",
          beforeSend: function () {
              var load = $('<div id="load"><p>Loading data...</p></
    div>');
              load.appendTo('body');
          },
          complete: function () {
            $('#load').remove();
          },
        success: function (data) {
          var table = $('#dynamicTable');
           var trthead = $('<tr/>');
           var head = $('<thead/>');
           trthead.appendTo(head);
           //Loop over the columns
                $.each(data.listColumns, function (index, value) {
           var column = $('<th>' + value.Title + '</th>');
           trthead.append(column);
                });
           var tbody = $('<tbody/>');
           //Loop over the rows;
           for (var i = 0; i < data.listRows.length; i++) {
                var tr = $('<tr/>');
           for (var t = 0; t < data.listRows[i].Value.length; t++) {
            if(t == 0){
            tr.append('<th>' + data.listRows[i].Value[t] + '</th>');
             }else{
            tr.append('<td>' + data.listRows[i].Value[t] + '</td>');}
            }
```

```
        tbody.append(tr);
        }
        table.append(head);
          table.append(tbody);
    },
      error: function (xhr, er) {
        $('body').html('<p>Sorry! Something wrong happened.')

      }
  });
```

 You can read more about Ajax requests using jQuery at
http://api.jquery.com/jQuery.ajax.

Converting tables into graphs (Advanced)

Another alternative much discussed by the community of developers is transforming the table into a graphic when it is being displayed on small screen devices. This is not an easy task taking into account the size and amount of data that a table can have.

Let's see an alternative solution combining the previous recipes with another plugin for rendering graphics. The main reason for this combination is we use only one plugin per page, thus optimizing our load.

Getting ready

We maintained the same structure for our table, however this time we do not use this example and load it via AJAX. So the markup looks as follows, code example, *Chapter06_Codes_1*:

```
<table id="dynamicTable" class="table">
    <thead>
        <tr>
          <th>Reviews</th>
          <th>Top</th>
          <th>Rolling Stones</th>
          <th>Rock Hard</th>
          <th>Kerrang</th>
        </tr>
    </thead>
    <tbody>
        <tr>
          <th>Ac/Dc</th>
          <td>10</td>
```

```
      <td>9</td>
      <td>8</td>
      <td>9</td>
    </tr>
    <tr>
      <th>Queen</th>
      <td>9</td>
      <td>6</td>
      <td>8</td>
      <td>5</td>
    </tr>
    <tr>
      <th>Whitesnake</th>
      <td>8</td>
      <td>9</td>
      <td>8</td>
      <td>6</td>
    </tr>
    <tr>
      <th>Deep Purple</th>
      <td>10</td>
      <td>6</td>
      <td>9</td>
      <td>8</td>
    </tr>
    <tr>
      <th>Black Sabbath</th>
      <td>10</td>
      <td>5</td>
      <td>7</td>
      <td>8</td>
    </tr>
  </tbody>
</table>
```

How to do it...

Let's see what we need to do:

1. Add a div right on the top of our table with an ID called `graph`:

   ```
   <div id="graph"></div>
   ```

2. We will use a jQuery Plugin called Highcharts, which can be downloaded for free from `http://www.highcharts.com/products/highcharts`.

3. Add the following script to the bottom of our document:

```
<script src="highcharts.js"></script>
```

4. Add a simple script to initialize the graph as follows:

```
var chart;
Highcharts.visualize = function(table, options) {
    // the data series
    options.series = [];
    var l= options.series.length;
    options.series[l] = {
        name: $('thead th:eq('+(l+1)+')', table).text(),
        data: []
    };
    $('tbody tr', table).each( function(i) {
        var tr = this;
        var th = $('th', tr).text();
        var td = parseFloat($('td', tr).text());
        options.series[0].data.push({name:th,y:td});
    });
    chart = new Highcharts.Chart(options);
}
// On document ready, call visualize on the datatable.
$(document).ready(function() {

    var table = document.getElementById('dynamicTable'),
    options = {
            chart: {
                renderTo: 'graph',
                defaultSeriesType: 'pie'
            },
            title: {
                text: 'Review Notes from Metal Mags'
            },
            plotOptions: {
                pie: {
                    allowPointSelect: true,
                    cursor: 'pointer',
                    dataLabels: {
                        enabled: false
                    },
                    showInLegend: true
                }
            },
```

```
            tooltip: {
                pointFormat: 'Total: <b>{point.percentage}%</
b>',
                percentageDecimals: 1
            }
        };

    Highcharts.visualize(table, options);
});
```

Many people choose to hide the div with the table in smaller devices and show only the graph.

Once they've optimized our table and depending on the amount of data, there is no problem. It also shows that the choice is yours.

5. Now when we look at the browser, we can view both the table and the graph as shown in the following screenshot:

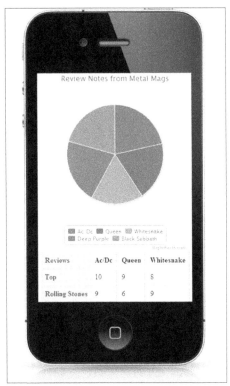

Browser screenshot at 320px.

Highcharts plugins have an excellent quality in all browsers and works with SVG, they are compatible with iPad, iPhone, and IE 6.

How it works...

The plugin can generate the table using only a single data array, but by our intuition and step-by-step description of its uses, we have created the following code to generate the graph starting from a table previously created.

We create the graph using the id#= dynamicTable function, where we read its contents through the following function:

```
$('tbody tr', table).each( function(i) {
        var tr = this;
        var th = $('th', tr).text();
        var td = parseFloat($('td', tr).text());
        options.series[0].data.push({name:th,y:td});
    });
```

In the plugin settings, we set the div graph to receive the graph after it is rendered by the script. We also add a pie type and a title for our graph.

```
options = {
        chart: {
                renderTo: 'graph',
                defaultSeriesType: 'pie'
        },
        title: {
                text: 'Review Notes from Metal Mags'
        },
```

There's more...

We can hide the table using media query so that only the graph appears. Remember that it just hides the fact and does not prevent it from being loaded by the browser; however we still need it to build the graph.

For this, just apply display none to the table inside the breakpoint:

```
@media only screen and (max-width: 768px) {

    .table { display: none; }
}
```

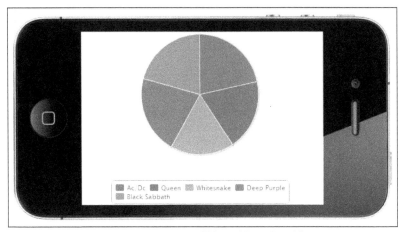

Browser screenshot at 320px, without the table

Merging data – numbers and text (Advanced)

We introduce an alternative based on CSS3 for dealing with tables containing text and numbers.

Getting ready

Tables are used for different purposes, we will see an example where our data is not a data table. (Code Example: *Chapter07_Codes_1*)

CONTACT	Manager	Label	Phone
Black Sabbath	Richard Both	Atlantic	+1 (408) 257-1500
Ac/DC	Paolla Matazo	Sony	+1 (302) 236-0800
Queen	Suzane Yeld	Warner	+1 (103) 222-6754
Whitesnake	Paul S. Senne	Vertigo	+1 (456) 233-1243
Deep Purple	Ian Friedman	CosaNostra	+1 (200) 255-0066

Browser screenshot at 1024px

Although our table did not have many columns, showing it on a small screen is not easy. Hence we will progressively show the change in the table by subtracting the width of the screen.

How to do it...

Note that we have removed the `.table` class so this time apply the style directly in the table tags, see the following steps:

1. Let's use a simple table structure as we saw before.

2. Add some CSS3 to make some magic with our selectors.

3. Set our breakpoints to two sizes.

```
<table>
    <thead>
      <tr>
      <th>CONTACT</th>
      <th scope="col">Manager</th>
      <th scope="col">Label</th>
      <th scope="col">Phone</th>
      </tr>
    </thead>
    <tbody>
      <tr>
        <th scope="row">Black Sabbath</th>
        <td>Richard Both</td>
        <td>Atlantic</td>
        <td>+1 (408) 257-1500 </td>
      </tr>
      <tr>
        <th scope="row">Ac/DC</th>
        <td>Paolla Matazo</td>
        <td>Sony</td>
        <td>+1 (302) 236-0800</td>
      </tr>
      <tr>
        <th scope="row">Queen</th>
        <td>Suzane Yeld</td>
        <td>Warner</td>
        <td>+1 (103) 222-6754</td>
      </tr>
      <tr>
        <th scope="row">Whitesnake</th>
        <td>Paul S. Senne</td>
        <td>Vertigo</td>
        <td>+1 (456) 233-1243</td>
      </tr>
      <tr>
        <th scope="row">Deep Purple</th>
```

```
        <td>Ian Friedman</td>
        <td>CosaNostra</td>
        <td>+1 (200) 255-0066</td>
      </tr>
  </tbody>
</table>
```

4. Applying the style as follows:

```
table {
     width: 100%;
     background-color: transparent;
     border-collapse: collapse;
     border-spacing: 0;
     background-color: #fff
 }
 th {
   text-align: left;
 }
 td:last-child, th:last-child {
   text-align:right;
 }
 td, th {
   padding: 6px 12px;
 }
 tr:nth-child(odd), tr:nth-child(odd) {
   background: #f3f3f3;
 }
 tr:nth-child(even) {
   background: #ebebeb;
 }
 thead tr:first-child, thead tr:first-child {
   background: #000;
   color:white;
 }
 table td:empty {
   background:white;
 }
```

5. We use CSS3 pseudo-selectors here again to help in the transformation of the table. And the most important part, the Media Queries breakpoints:

```
@media (max-width: 768px) {
     tr :nth-child(3) {display: none;}
 }
```

```
@media (max-width: 480px) {
  thead tr:first-child {display: none;}
  th {display: block}
  td {display: inline!important;}
}
```

6. When the resolution is set to 768px, we note that the penultimate column is removed.

CONTACT	Manager	Phone
Black Sabbath	Richard Both	+1 (408) 257-1500
Ac/DC	Paolla Matazo	+1 (302) 236-0800
Queen	Suzane Yeld	+1 (103) 222-6754
Whitesnake	Paul S. Senne	+1 (456) 233-1243
Deep Purple	Ian Friedman	+1 (200) 255-0066

This way we keep the most relevant information on the screen. We have hidden the information less relevant to the subject. And when we decrease further, we have the data distributed as a block.

Mixing everything – texts, numbers, and more data (Advanced)

So far, during our examples we have seen several alternatives to deal with our tables, from simple CSS-based solutions to the use of JavaScript and some jQuery plugins.

We also saw how to convert our table into graph and several tips on how we can optimize its appearance in various screen sizes. Now we bring an extreme alternative, let's completely transform our table to use `<div>` elements.

Getting ready

Let's now use the jQuery method, `replaceWith ()`, to make the transformation of the table's elements to div elements. (Code example: *Chapter08_Codes_1*)

More information about this method can be found here: `http://api.jquery.com/replaceWith`

The following screenshot shows how our table looks on this browser:

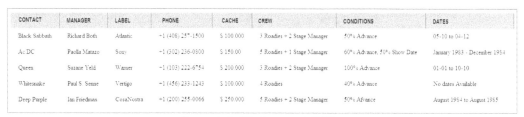

CONTACT	MANAGER	LABEL	PHONE	CACHE	CREW	CONDITIONS	DATES
Black Sabbath	Richard Both	Atlantic	+1 (408) 257-1500	$ 100.000	3 Roadies + 2 Stage Manager	50% Advance	05-10 to 04-12
AcDC	Paolla Matazo	Sony	+1 (302) 236-0800	$ 150.00	5 Roadies + 1 Stage Manager	60% Advance, 50% Show Date	January 1983 - December 1984
Queen	Suzane Yeld	Warner	+1 (103) 222-6754	$ 200.000	3 Roadies + 2 Stage Manager	100% Advance	01-01 to 10-10
Whitesnake	Paul S. Senne	Vertigo	+1 (456) 233-1243	$ 100.000	4 Roadies	40% Advance	No dates Available
Deep Purple	Ian Friedman	CosaNostra	+1 (200) 255-0066	$ 250.000	5 Roadies + 2 Stage Manager	50% Afvance	August 1984 to August 1985

Screenshot of the browser at 1024px

How to do it...

We keep the same semantic table structure. Still we make use of the CSS3 pseudo-classes to help us with the style of the table. In our stylesheet we are using classes as `.row` and `.column` that are currently not in our markup.

1. Add more style to Media Query breakpoint.

2. Add the JavaScript to complete the task.

3. Let's have a hands on experience:

```
<table class="table">
    <thead>
      <tr>
        <th scope="column"></th>
      </tr>
```

```
        </thead>
        <tbody>
          <tr>
            <th scope="row"></th>
            <td></td>
          </tr>
        </tbody>
      </table>
```

4. Add the additional CSS as follows:

```
.table{
  display:table;
  border-bottom:2px solid #dddddd;
  margin:10px 0;
  width:100%;
}
.table-head{
    display: table-header-group;
}
.table-head .column {
  background:#333333;
  color:#7d7d7d;
  border-right:1px solid #5d5d5d;
  border-bottom:none;
}
.table-head .column:hover{
  background:#222222;
}
.row{
  display:table-row;
}
.row .column:nth-child(1){
  border-left:1px solid #eeeeee;
}
.row:last-child .column{
  border-bottom:none;
}
.column{
  display:table-cell;
  padding:10px 20px;
  border-bottom:1px solid #eeeeee;
  border-right:1px solid #eeeeee;
}
```

```css
.column:hover{
  background:#f9f9f9;
}
```

5. And finally add our Media Query as follows:

```css
@media all and (max-width: 768px){
  .table,
  .row,
  .column,
  .column:before{
    display:block;
  }
  .table,
  .row .column:last-child{
    border-bottom:none;
  }
  .table-head{
    position:absolute;
    top:-1000em;
    left:-1000em;
  }
  .row{
    border:1px solid #eee;
    border-top:2px solid #ddd;
    border-bottom:2px solid #ddd;
    margin:20px 0;
  }
  .row .column:nth-child(1){
    border-left:none;
  }
  .row .column:last-child{
    border-right:none;
  }
  .row:last-child .column,
  .column{
    border-bottom:1px solid #eeeeee;
  }
  .column:before{
    font-weight:bold;
    padding-right:20px;
    font-size:12px;
    content:" "attr(data-label)" :";
  }
}
```

6. Now the magic happens in our JavaScript, when we use the `replaceWith()` method:

```javascript
var headCol =  $('thead th').size();
  for ( i=0; i <= headCol; i++ )   {
    var headColLabel = $('thead th:nth-child('+ i +')').text();
    $('tr th:nth-child('+ i +')').replaceWith(
      function(){
        return $('<div class="column" data-label="'+ headColLabel
+'">').append($(this).contents());
      }
    );
      $('tr td:nth-child('+ i +')').replaceWith(
        function(){
          return $('<div class="column" data-label="'+
headColLabel +'">').append($(this).contents());
        }
      );
  }
  $('table').replaceWith(
    function(){
      return $('<div class="table">').append($(this).contents());
    }
  );
  $('thead').replaceWith(
    function(){
      return $('<div class="table-head">').append($(this).
contents());
    }
  );
  $('tr').replaceWith(
    function(){
      return $('<div class="row">').append($(this).contents());
    }
  );
  $('th').replaceWith(
    function(){
      return $('<div class="column">').append($(this).contents());
    }
  );
```

7. Now when we resize our browser, all the table elements that we see before changed to div elements. Take a look at the result after the DOM is ready:

```html
<div class="table">
      <div class="table-head">
        <div class="row">
```

```
        <div class="column" data-label="CONTACT">CONTACT</div>
        <div class="column" data-label="Manager">Manager</div>
      </div>
    </div>
    <tbody>
      <div class="row">
        <div class="column" data-label="CONTACT">Black Sabbath</
div>
        <div class="column" data-label="Manager">Richard Both</
div>
      </div>
    </tbody>
</div>
```

The result on browser after resizing:

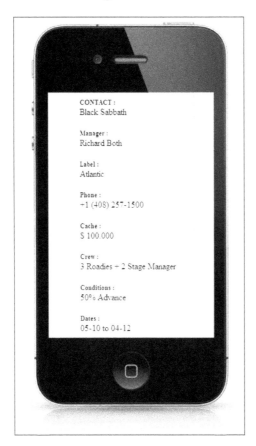

As you can see, we transform table rows into divs and add the contents of our table.

Thank you for buying
Instant HTML5 Responsive Table Design How-to

About Packt Publishing

Packt, pronounced 'packed', published its first book "*Mastering phpMyAdmin for Effective MySQL Management*" in April 2004 and subsequently continued to specialize in publishing highly focused books on specific technologies and solutions.

Our books and publications share the experiences of your fellow IT professionals in adapting and customizing today's systems, applications, and frameworks. Our solution based books give you the knowledge and power to customize the software and technologies you're using to get the job done. Packt books are more specific and less general than the IT books you have seen in the past. Our unique business model allows us to bring you more focused information, giving you more of what you need to know, and less of what you don't.

Packt is a modern, yet unique publishing company, which focuses on producing quality, cutting-edge books for communities of developers, administrators, and newbies alike. For more information, please visit our website: www.packtpub.com.

Writing for Packt

We welcome all inquiries from people who are interested in authoring. Book proposals should be sent to author@packtpub.com. If your book idea is still at an early stage and you would like to discuss it first before writing a formal book proposal, contact us; one of our commissioning editors will get in touch with you.

We're not just looking for published authors; if you have strong technical skills but no writing experience, our experienced editors can help you develop a writing career, or simply get some additional reward for your expertise.

HTML5 Mobile Development Cookbook

ISBN: 978-1-84969-196-3   Paperback: 254 pages

Over 60 recipes for building fast, responsive HTML5 mobile websites for iPhone 5, Android, Windows Phone, and Blackberry

1. Solve your cross platform development issues by implementing device and content adaptation recipes.

2. Maximum action, minimum theory allowing you to dive straight into HTML5 mobile web development.

3. Incorporate HTML5-rich media and geo-location into your mobile websites.

HTML5 Multimedia Development Cookbook

ISBN: 978-1-84969-104-8   Paperback: 288 pages

Recipes for practical, real-world HTML5 multimedia-driven development

1. Use HTML5 to enhance JavaScript functionality. Display videos dynamically and create movable ads using jQuery.

2. Set up the canvas environment, process shapes dynamically and create interactive visualizations.

3. Enhance accessibility by testing browser support, providing alternative site views and displaying alternate content for non supported browsers.

Please check **www.PacktPub.com** for information on our titles

Responsive Web Design with HTML5 and CSS3

ISBN: 978-1-84969-318-9   Paperback: 324 pages

Learn responsive design using HTML5 and CSS3 to adapt websites to any browser or screen size

1. Everything needed to code websites in HTML5 and CSS3 that are responsive to every device or screen size

2. Learn the main new features of HTML5 and use CSS3's stunning new capabilities including animations, transitions and transformations

3. Real world examples show how to progressively enhance a responsive design while providing fall backs for older browsers

HTML5 Boilerplate Web Development

ISBN: 978-1-84951-850-5   Paperback: 174 pages

Master Web Development with a robust set of templates to get your projects done quickly and effectively

1. Master HTML5 Boilerplate as starting templates for future projects

2. Learn how to optimize your workflow with HTML5 Boilerplate templates and set up servers optimized for performance

3. Learn to feature-detect and serve appropriate styles and scripts across browser types

Please check **www.PacktPub.com** for information on our titles

www.ingramcontent.com/pod-product-compliance
Lightning Source LLC
LaVergne TN
LVHW080105070326
832902LV00014B/2434

* 9 7 8 1 8 4 9 6 9 7 2 6 2 *